ci m 1

Also in the *From Stage to Print* series:

A White Rose at Midnight by Lim Chor Pee
Mimi Fan by Lim Chor Pee
Fear of Writing by Tan Tarn How
Those Who Can't, Teach by Haresh Sharma
Everything But the Brain by Jean Tay
Boom by Jean Tay

Playwright Omnibus series:

Six Plays by Desmond Sim
Student Plays by Desmond Sim
Four Plays by Chong Tze Chien
Eight Plays by Ovidia Yu
Six Plays by Tan Tarn How

model citizens

a play by haresh sharma

EPIGRAM BOOKS / SINGAPORE

Copyright © 2012 by The Necessary Stage
Introduction copyright © 2012 by Alvin Tan

All rights reserved.

Published in Singapore by
Epigram Books
www.epigrambooks.sg

National Library Board, Singapore
Cataloguing-in-Publication Data

Sharma, Haresh.
Model citizens : a play / Haresh Sharma.
– Singapore : Epigram, 2012.
p. cm.
ISBN : 978-981-07-1461-1 (pbk.)

1. Singapore – Drama. 2. Women – Drama. I. Title.

PR9570.S53
S822 -- dc22   OCN776769919

This is a work of fiction. Names, characters, places, and incidents either are the product of the author's imagination or are used fictitiously. Any resemblance to actual persons, living or dead, events, or locales is entirely coincidental.

First Edition
10 9 8 7 6 5 4 3 2

PERFORMING RIGHTS

Professionals and amateur groups wishing to stage this play or perform a public reading of it must get written permission from The Necessary Stage, 278 Marine Parade Road #B1-02 Marine Parade Community Building, Singapore 449282 (www.necessary.org).

CONTENTS

	Introduction by Alvin Tan	ix
	Production Notes	xv
	Characters	xvii
	ACT 1	1
SCENE 1	Day 1	3
SCENE 2	Day 1	8
SCENE 3	Day 2	12
SCENE 4	Three weeks ago	20
	ACT 2	29
SCENE 1	Day 2	31
SCENE 2	Day 14	37
SCENE 3	Six months ago	44
	ACT 3	49
SCENE 1	Day 30	51
SCENE 2	Day 40	60
SCENE 3	Day 50	63
	About the Playwright	76
	About the The Necessary Stage	77
	About the Publisher	78

MODEL CITIZENS: CELEBRATING DIFFERENCE
Introduction by Alvin Tan

In the era of the global village, there seems to be more bigotry, intolerance and hatred than inclusiveness, understanding and compassion. What is really happening on the ground in our daily lives?

There are many factors responsible for ethnic tension and for people failing to co-exist or engage in meaningful interaction with one another.

Foremost, there is increased mobility today with more people travelling for work and leisure, and settling, temporarily or permanently, outside their birth land. Borders become less consequential as we intermingle and as countries compete to attract talent and skilled labour to remain ahead.

This dilution of borders is very well the result of imperative and pragmatic economic goals, but often, insufficient priority is given to the appreciation of different cultural sensibilities of day-to-day matters. Over time, ignorance and prejudice grow and eventually become entrenched in our understanding or perception of the 'other'.

In addition, with power, difference is often politicised rather than celebrated. Power often determines how values from a dominant culture may permeate the body politic and go on to shape sensibilities and perspectives, which, over time, may become institutionalised. As policies are formulated and implemented, one ethnic group may become privileged while another diminished in significance. This is because power works to preserve the status quo, and the traditional hierarchical structure is usually more accepted or preferred than concentric circles of multiple power centres (i.e. co-existence), minority groups frequently end up negotiating with the dominant.

The culture of hierarchical power must be challenged if we aspire to make way for spaces sympathetic to collaborative impulses, where different cultural sensibilities exist more equitably and may therefore permutate freely and fuse meaningfully.

For instance, although a country may claim to be meritocratic, the criteria or premise upon which merit is determined is not necessarily independent of cultural values. This is especially true if class is also perceived as a cultural category.

The danger is that instead of respecting differences or engaging with elements from other cultures to forge new identities and relations, we may develop cultural insecurities or a purist mindset, or both, which can lead to ethnocentric dispositions and discriminatory outcomes.

How then do we reflect on how governmental policies affect our lives? How should we construct our attitudes towards one another and towards the society we are in the process of becoming?

I believe one of the ways is to nurture spaces where the contestation of different cultural perspectives may take place. These spaces, which are already hosted by theatre, the arts, new media and civil society—where citizens are able to debate, discourse and discover issues and ideas without fear—should be encouraged to flourish. These spaces should not be regulated or policed, or anyone persecuted, as they are potential powerhouses for addressing present-day maladies.

We need to have faith, trust and respect. We need to subdue the paranoia that the worst-case scenario, such as social unrest, will come true. We need to stop nipping things in the bud. Instead, we should trust citizens to engage in non-violent, albeit passionate, debate and believe that conflict can inspire new insights. Difference is celebrated when we tap from our very own diversity to strengthen social cohesion organically. In this way we might re-imagine our destiny as a young nation making real progress.

At present, although some countries may appear cosmopolitan and multicultural, their environments are really more nationalist-oriented than intercultural. To move forward, we have to acknowledge the limitations of yesterday's multiculturalism. Multiculturalism is a limited instrument in that it is merely a recognition of different cultures. On the other hand, interculturalism, which refers to the interaction of different cultures (sensibilities, beliefs or perspectives), encourages openness and the interplay of different cultural presences in an environment where relationships are governed by mutual respect, deep appreciation and even admiration.

In Singapore, intercultural outcomes would be similar to the hybridised Peranakan (Straits-born) and Eurasian cultures. Such possibilities contrast starkly with what is found in Japan, where one cannot become Japanese; one can only be born Japanese. As nationality is not tied up with ethnicity, Singapore offers a space where citizens' identities remain fluid, heterogenous and open.

On the other hand, nationalism if gone overboard can easily be evangelical in that it shows little or no respect for the beliefs of others. It is adequate perhaps only enough for residents to co-exist but not enough to intermingle. It can denigrate or negate other beliefs in favour of the one it propagates. The question is, is ultra-nationalism inevitable and immutable, and would it therefore always exist to enlarge the gap in human relations? Or are we capable of transcending the fault lines of nationality, race and religion with measured compassion and start building bridges?

How do we value purity? Is purity more or less important when we consider identity in today's world without borders? Is homogeneity a strength, a right or a choice, or are categories such as heterogeneity, diversity and hybridisation more appropriate? Will fragmentation make for a better world or will it heighten the possibilities for more tension, quarrels, cultural unrest and wars?

When I think of the phrase 'model citizens', I am prompted to ask: What am I looking at? What citizenship are we addressing here? What is this reality we 'belong' to? Would there not be an array of modes and modulations when we take into account the rate and range of intercultural interactions occurring in a world without borders? Indeed, how do we prepare ourselves to be citizens of contemporary realities? We have to quarrel to converge. We have to engage in conflict to synthesise. We have to debate to transcend.

These were the challenges we were constantly confronted with throughout the process of putting *Model Citizens*, the play, together. From our numerous improvisations, we eventually selected three characters from different historical and socio-cultural backgrounds for further development: an MP's wife (an ex-Nantah graduate), an Indonesian maid and her Peranakan employer—and a story slowly emerged.

The story also provided a framework that propelled the journeys of the three characters and their relationships. Haresh has skillfully crafted nuanced interactions of their respective worldviews in dynamic contestation and negotiation, such that an intercultural narrative—powerful, poignant, relevant and insightful—unfolds to an audience still new to the political potential of cross-cultural theatre that interrogates our contemporary realities.

As Mahatma Gandhi put it: "I do not want to foresee the future. I am concerned with taking care of the present. God has given me no control over the moment following."

Model Citizens is a microcosm of people relating across cultures, an exploration of the politics of language, class and difference. It is imperative that we continue this struggle in full respect and appreciation of our present needs. It is urgent that we scrutinise how differences are confronted and facilitated.

Alvin Tan, 2012
Founder and Artistic Director, The Necessary Stage

PRODUCTION NOTES

Model Citizens was first performed by The Necessary Stage from 3 to 14 March 2010 at The Necessary Stage Black Box. It was restaged at the National Museum of Singapore Gallery Theatre from 11 to 15 January 2011 as part of the M1 Singapore Fringe Festival. The play toured to Kuala Lumpur from 19 to 22 January 2011 at the KL Performing Arts Centre.

The play was directed by Alvin Tan; set design by Vincent Lim; lighting design by Lim Woan Wen; and multimedia design by Mohd Fadlin bin Mohd Saffri. Translations were provided by Goh Guat Kian, Siti Khalijah Zainal, Sammaria Simanjuntak, Wong Chee Meng, Peggy Ferroa, and Melissa Lim.

The cast was as follows:

MRS CHUA	Goh Guat Kian
MELLY	Siti Khalijah Zainal
WENDY	Karen Tan

CHARACTERS

MRS CHUA   MP's wife, 55
MELLY   Indonesian maid, 24
WENDY   Melly's employer, 45

ACT 1

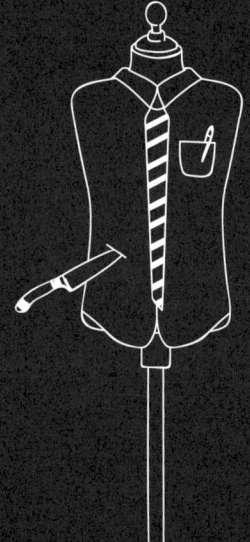

ACT 1 : SCENE 1

Day 1

Mrs Chua and Melly are together. Pause.
Mrs Chua laughs.

MRS CHUA 我知道我不应该大声笑… 但是我刚从医院回来。他因为药物的作用, 连话都说不清楚。我从来没有看过他这个样子。
[I know I shouldn't be laughing… but I just came from the hospital. He couldn't speak properly because he was heavily medicated. Never seen him like that before.]

Pause. Mrs Chua laughs.

MRS CHUA 你男朋友为什么想杀他?
[Why did your boyfriend want to kill him?]

MELLY Hah?

MRS CHUA You… talk Chinese?

MELLY …

MRS CHUA You maid. Work maid.

MELLY Yes. I… Three years. Work here.

MRS CHUA Indo…

MELLY Yes. I Indonesia. Kamu bisa ngomong Bahasa Indonesia nggak?
[Yes. I Indonesia. Do you speak Bahasa Indonesia?]

MRS CHUA Hah? 哎呀! 怎么这样? 你听不懂我说什么。我也听不懂你讲什么。真是鸡同鸭讲。
[Hah? Aiyoh, what is this? You don't understand me. I don't understand you. Like duck and chicken…]

MELLY My boyfriend… he jail.

MRS CHUA Yes. Jail. He (*action of stabbing*) my husband.

MELLY No! He never (*action of stabbing*) your husband.

MRS CHUA My husband MP! Your boyfriend siow! Why he (*action of stabbing*) my husband?

MELLY I don't know. (*pause*) Auntie tolong…

MRS CHUA 我都不知道为什么会给你我的电话号码。看到你在法庭上…那样的看着他…那样的看着我…你很年轻。你知道你有多年轻吗？你知道男人…对的，男人会把你一生搞得乱七八糟？所以我叫我的司机跟你谈谈看你OK吗。这件事并不是你的错。他所做的这些跟你没有关系。你明白吗？(停顿) 你怎么会明白？你当然不会明白。连我都搞不懂我为什么要跟你说这些？

[I don't know why I gave you my phone number. When I saw you in the court room… the way you looked at him, the way you looked at me… You are so young. Do you know how young you are? Do you know how men can turn your life upside down? That's why I asked my driver to talk to you. To see if you are okay. This is not your fault. What he did is not your fault. You understand? (*slight pause*) How can you understand? Of course you don't understand. Why am I even talking to you?

Pause.

MELLY My name Melly. Maaf, tapi saya nggak bisa ngomong bahasa Cina. Bahasa Inggris saya juga tidak bagus. Saya beruntung karena Ma'am saya bisa ngomong bahasa Melayu. Saya suruh dia ngomong sama kamu? Dia orangnya baik. Dia kasi saya off, biar saya bisa bikin kerja lain. Saya telpon dia. Kamu ngomong sama dia OK? [My name Melly. I'm sorry but I cannot speak Chinese. Even my English is very bad. I'm very lucky because my Ma'am can speak Malay. I ask her to talk to you? She's very nice. She gives me time off, she lets me do other work. I call her. You talk to her okay?]

Melly takes out her mobile phone and makes a call.

MELLY Hello Ibu? Melly sini. Ibu bisa—
[Hello Ibu? It's Melly. Can you—]
She hangs up. Pause.

MRS CHUA Makan!

MELLY Makan?

MRS CHUA Makan. You want makan?

MELLY I... I don't... makan babi.

MRS CHUA No babi. I cook... mee.

MELLY Mee goreng?

MRS CHUA Mee sua.

Melly's phone rings. She answers. It is Wendy.

MELLY Hello? Ibu, Melly di rumah Mrs Chua. Tidak! Tidak... Melly telpon Mrs Chua karena—Nggak, Mrs Chua yang berikan Melly... Ibu bisa suruh Mrs Chua bantu?... Tapi dia di dalam jail dan Mrs Chua bisa— (*kepada Mrs Chua*) My boss...
[Hello? Ibu, I'm at Mrs Chua's house. No! No... I called her because—No, she gave me... Can you ask her to help?... But he's in jail and she can—(*to Mrs Chua*) My boss...]

Mrs Chua takes Melly's handphone.

MRS CHUA 哈罗？是，是我是蔡中进的太太…没有，没有问题。你不用道歉。谢谢，谢谢。他还在医院，不过他好多了…还好啦，她年轻…她要我帮忙，可是我什么都不能做。这已经是刑事案件了。也许你叫她忘记那男人…她很幸运有这样的一份好工作，还有你这样的好雇主…不用客气，真的，没有问题。谢谢你的问候。

[Yes, I am Chua Chong Jin's wife… No need to apologise. Thank you. He's getting better. Still at the hospital… It's okay, she's young… She wants my help but I cannot do anything. It's a court case now. Maybe you tell her to just forget about him… just be grateful she has a good job, a good employer like you… No, please, it's really not a problem… Thank you for your kind wishes…]

Mrs Chua gives the phone to Melly. She goes to get some food.

MELLY Yah… Iya… Tapi bagaimana kalau dia tidak bisa dilepaskan jail? …Tapi mengapa? Dia kan isterinya. Dia bisa bantu. Dia bisa beritahu suaminya, suruh suaminya bantu. Tanya saja sama dia, ngomong saja sama dia. Tolong… Dia kan punya kuasa. Mereka pasti dengar katanya. Melly sudah tidak ada apa-apa lagi untuk terus hidup. Tolong bantulah, tolong… ini untuk kehidupan Melly, masa depan Melly. Dia—

[Yes… Yes… But what if he can't get out of jail?… But why? She's his wife. She can help.

She can ask her husband to help. Just ask him, just speak with him. Please... He has the power. They'll listen to him. I have nothing else to live for. Please help, please...this is my life, my future. He's—]

Melly keeps her phone. Pause.

MRS CHUA You makan? Mee sua? No babi.

Pause. She gives a bowl of noodles to Melly, who eats.

MRS CHUA 我知道你很害怕。我知道你爱他,你想念他。你要和他在一起。但是,我这是在保护你。一切都会没事。不要想不开。来吃点东西。然后回家去... 好好的过日子。

[I know you're frightened. I know you love him. You miss him. You want to be with him. But I'm protecting you. Everything will be fine. Don't be sad. Have something to eat. Then you can go back home... and carry on with your life.]

Pause. Mrs Chua laughs.

MRS CHUA Thinking my husband...

ACT 1 : SCENE 2

Day 1

Wendy is reading a saved online conversation between her son Tony (nick: angel) and an anonymous friend (nick: shishi).

SHISHI   Hey, fucker, what you doing? Long time no see you.

ANGEL   I writing song.

SHISHI   WTF!!! ROTFL!!!

ANGEL   Nah beh... I writing song about Au Sang Suu Kyi. Gonna sing at Speaker's corner.

SHISHI   You kana tangkap damn go to jail sia.

ANGEL   I fight injustice mah

SHISHI   You blardy in love with her. She's your goddess. LOL.

ANGEL   Wei! The Juntah are damn fuckers liow.

SHISHI   Fren, you are fucking Sporean. Act like 1.

ANGEL   F Spore.

SHISHI   LOL Migrate lor.

Pause. Her phone rings. She answers.

WENDY   Lu mo' apa[1], Margaret? I said I'm fine. You don't have to call every day just to check... What is that supposed to mean? I'll go back to work when I feel like it. What's it to you? Lu mo' gua buat apa? Nangis sempai mata jatoh?[2] (*slight pause*) No! Don't come... and don't you dare bring Ji Ee, Sa Ee and Ee Ee Bulat—Margaret, eh, tunggu, tunggu, I have another call. (*pause*) Hello?... Melly, I'm on the other line. (*pause*) What does the family want me to do? Invite everyone over and have a press conference?...

---

1   lu mo' apa [*Bahasa Indonesia*] What do you want?
2   lu mo' gua buat apa? Nangis sempai mata jatoh? [*Bahasa Indonesia*] What do you want me to do? Cry my eyes out?

Bullshit, they want to show support. They just want to gossip. I don't care what they accuse me of. I have no time for them.

She hangs up. She continues reading.

ANGEL   LOL!!! ROTFL!!!

SHISHI   Wat so funny?

ANGEL   My mum swearing at the Chinese workers next door. She think I not at home. She say F them LOL!!!

SHISHI   Crazy family. You at home and yr mum dun even noe. My parents damn strict. That's why I internet at library.

ANGEL   What library?

SHISHI   Che! I donno you, you donno me. No need to ask.

ANGEL   You my chat buddy mah.

SHISHI   Yah, e-buddy LOL.

Pause. She calls Melly.

WENDY   Apa pasal Melly?... siapa punya rumah? Lu gila ka? Lu balek skarang!... Lu macam mana cari dia punya rumah?... Tok sa, lu balek skarang... Gua cakap sama dia.

[What is it Melly?... whose house? Are you crazy? Leave right now!... How did you find her house?... Never mind, come home now... Pass the phone to her.]

Pause.

WENDY   Hello? 你是MP的太太吗？我的工人麻烦你，真对不起。你的先生好吗…我真的对不起。OK, OK, 我告诉她。请原谅我。祝你的先生快点好起来。

[Hello? You are the MP's wife?... I am very sorry about my maid... I hope your husband is well... I am very sorry... Yes, yes, I will tell her that. Again, please accept my deepest apologies. And please wish your husband a speedy recovery.]

Pause.

WENDY Lu balek skarang. Dia tak boleh buat apa apa. Cakap apa sama Sir? Jangan minta lagi. Biarkan dia!

[Come back. There's nothing she can do... Speak with him about what?... Stop begging and leave her alone!]

She hangs up. She continues reading.

ANGEL Can I ask something. You M or F?
SHISHI Wah liao! Why so emo?
ANGEL Me M
SHISHI CB. Use that kind of Nick.
ANGEL I Angel wat.
SHISHI Yah. My f-ing guardian Angel.
ANGEL Soon I will be.
SHISHI What U mean?
ANGEL Nothing...You M or F?
SHISHI Don't be an idiot.
ANGEL I am Angel wat. An angel.
SHISHI Seriously... What do u mean?
SHISHI I'm not kidding.
SHISHI What do you mean guardian angel and all that?
SHISHI Angel?
SHISHI Do you want to talk? I'm F.
SHISHI Angel?
ANGEL ROTFL!!!

	SHISHI	CB.
	ANGEL	Come to Speaker's Corner. We can meet.
		You chio bu or not?
	SHISHI	FU! Hope you rot in jail!
		Pause.
	WENDY	I can't do this any more, Tony. I just can't…
		Pause. Wendy makes a call.
	WENDY	Lu masih di rumah Mrs Chua ka?… (*jeda*) Nanti, gua cakap sama dia besok… Lu jangan khuatir. Gua selesehkan.
		[Are you still at Mrs Chua's house?… (*slight pause*) I'll speak to her tomorrow. You don't worry. I will take care of it.]

ACT 1 : SCENE 3

Day 2

Mrs Chua and Wendy are together. They speak in Mandarin and Hokkien.

WENDY	你是怎么认识你的丈夫？
	[How did you meet your husband?]
MRS CHUA	在南大。
	[Nantah.]
WENDY	(*in Hokkien*) Eh, hee eh mm see kam liao?
	[Oh? Nanyang University. It was shut down right?]
MRS CHUA	(*in Hokkien*) Oh, ler dui Nantah gor jiah wu heng chu hor.
	[You seem very interested in Nantah.]
WENDY	(*in Hokkien*) Pai sei…
	[Sorry…]
MRS CHUA	他是个学生领袖…常常招惹麻烦。他常常梦想成为一个自由捍卫者。
	[He was a student leader… always getting into trouble. He always dreamt of being a freedom fighter.]
WENDY	Sorry, do you speak English? At all?
MRS CHUA	…
WENDY	Were you born in China?
MRS CHUA	No. No. I… born here.
WENDY	You CAN speak English.
MRS CHUA	No. No. I… my English no good.
WENDY	Well, it sounds perfect to me. For a Chinese ed. I'm Peranakan…

ACT 1 : SCENE 3

MRS CHUA Mrs…
WENDY Wendy.
MRS CHUA Mrs Wendy… excuse me…
Mrs Chua exits. Pause. Wendy walks around.
WENDY (*in Hokkien*) Ler eh chu jin sui.
[You have a very nice house.]
MRS CHUA (*offstage, in Hokkien*) Bo xi mi… 有点乱。
[It's nothing… very messy.]
WENDY 我住在HDB。HDB有很多benefits。有benefits, 有upgrading, rebate。我只要打电话，他们就会来丢垃圾，打扫corridor, 换灯泡。那些工人很好。从Indonesia, Bangladesh, Sri Lanka 也有… 很有礼貌。很不错。你应该是很满意，你现在什么都有了。你已经得到你的梦想了。
[I live in an HDB flat. HDB has a lot of benefits. Upgrading… rebate… I make one phone call and they will come. Clear the rubbish, clean the corridor… fix the light… The workers are very nice, very polite. From Indonesia, Bangladesh… even Sri Lanka. Very decent. You must be very proud. To have everything. To have fulfilled your dreams.
MRS CHUA (*offstage*) 这不算什么。
[It's nothing.]
WENDY 你的先生那么成功。你的孩子也都长大了。
(*in Hokkien*) Ler jin ho mia.
[Your husband is successful. Your children are grown up. You must have a good life.]
MRS CHUA (*offstage*) 谢谢。
[Thank you.]

1	WENDY	(*to herself*) Do you have a good life?
		Mrs Chua enters.
	MRS CHUA	对不起…
		[Sorry…]
5	WENDY	你说你的先生以前想做个 freedom fighter。他现在是个 MP。那你呢？你以前有什么梦想吗？
		[You said your husband dreamt of being a freedom fighter. And now he's an MP. What about you? What did you always dream of?]
10	MRS CHUA	从来没有人问过我这个问题。(停顿) 也许我年轻的时候曾经有过梦想和志愿。也许我也想成为一名自由捍卫者。甚至参与政治。但是后来我成为一名教师。
		[No one has ever asked me that. (*slight pause*)
15		Maybe I had dreams and aspirations when I was young. Maybe I too wanted to be a freedom fighter. Or maybe join politics. But I became a teacher.]
	WENDY	Chinese teacher?
20	MRS CHUA	Science.
	WENDY	Science.
	MRS CHUA	我用华语教了五年。直到那一天… 他们跟我说要用英语来教学。那时候大概只有三个月的时间让我把所有的课程换成英文。只有三个月。
25		我怎么用英语说"质量和速度的乘积等于力"，我怎么用英语说"作用力和反作用力是相等于，但方向相反"？
		[I taught in Chinese. For five years. Until one day… when I was told I had to teach in English.
30		I had about three months to change all my

lessons into English. Three months. How do I say "Force equals mass times acceleration" in English? How do I say "To every action, there is an equal and opposite reaction"?]

WENDY   To every action, there is an equal and opposite reaction.

MRS CHUA   To every action, there is… an equal and opposite… direction.

Pause. Wendy walks away. They are in their own thoughts.

WENDY   To be honest, I've not been out of my house for some time. It's like I've been sleeping for months. I think I'm sick as well… I have to see a doctor just to talk. He asks me a lot of questions… Are you happy? Yes I am. Are you sure? Yes, I'm positive. You seem sad. Do I? Do you feel loved? Of course. Do you love your children? I would die for them. Do you love your husband? I would die for him. Do you love yourself? Yes. Do you blame yourself?

Pause.

MRS CHUA   他差点要死掉。我每天都得去ICU看他。很多人都来看他。什么人都来。我收到很慰问的信和卡片。他们都来看他。我觉得我像是在国会里。他们都坐在里面。我要跟他们说…你还记得我吗？我出生在这里，这个国家。我生长在一个讲华语的家庭。我是个华校生。我还上了南大。在那里我认识了我的丈夫，还有了两个漂亮，天真的女儿。我的人生是那么的完美。然后你改变政策。你要我说英语。你要我停止生育，

你说两个就够了。你改变你的政策。你强迫我
动节育手术。现在你要大家多生孩子。你要大
家多生孩子。我想要生四个五个小孩,可是,
我得跟着你的政策。我跟着你所有的政策。
我听从、我服从、我把我自己投入你的政策,
然后你又改变你的政策。你又改变你的政策。
有谁会不恨你? 有谁会不想杀了你? (停顿) 那是
个在医院的国会,我能对他们说什么呢? 我什么
也不能说。

[He nearly died. Every day I had to go to the
ICU. Everyone came to see him. Everyone.
I have all the letters, all the cards… They all
came to see him. I felt like I was in parliament.
They were all there. I wanted to tell them…
Remember me? I was born here, in this
country. I was born speaking Chinese. I am
Chinese educated. I went to Nantah. I met my
husband and had children. Two beautiful,
innocent babies. My life was perfect. Then you
changed the rules. You wanted me to speak
English. You wanted me to stop having any
more children. Two is enough you said.
You changed the rules. You forced me to get
sterilised. Now you want more children.
I wanted more children. I wanted three or even
four. But I had to follow your rules. I followed
all your rules. I listened, I obeyed, I submitted
myself to your rules. And you just change them.
You just change the rules. Who wouldn't want
to hurt you? Who wouldn't want to kill you?

ACT 1 : SCENE 3

(*pause*) It was a parliament at the hospital. And I couldn't say anything. I couldn't even say anything.

Pause.

WENDY My kids used to love computer games when they were young. When I tell them to eat, they say wait. When I tell them to study, they say wait. When I tell them to shower, to sleep, to talk, to read… they say wait. I hate them. (*laughs*) Sometimes. But I shouldn't complain. I made them like that. I only realised it when I got my first maid. She was ironing their uniforms after dinner. My son came to me and said, "My shirt stinks." "No it doesn't." "It does. It stinks because that white thing she wears when she prays stinks as well. She's stinking all our clothes." My daughter went to the maid's room, took out her prayer garb and threw it at me. "See, it stinks!" (*pause*) She was nine years old… and I thought… how did I create these… monsters?

Pause.

MRS CHUA (*in Hokkien*) Ler hao seh eh dai ji, jin pai sei lah. [I'm very sorry about your son…]

WENDY (*in Hokkien*) Le eh sai pang mang gua eh gang lang eh da poh peng yu bo? Ler eh sai dao ka chiu bo?
[Can you help my maid's friend? Can you help her in any way?]

1	MRS CHUA	(*in Hokkien*) Wa zhun liong eh dao ka chiu. [I will try my best.]
	WENDY	其实,你什么也帮不了,对吗? [You can't do anything, can you?]
5	MRS CHUA	昨天你女佣来过之后,我和我的丈夫谈过了。他和警方也谈过。就算他不把他控上法庭也不行了——事情已经由不得他做主了。一旦犯了法,就得让警方…和法庭…做决定。
10		[After your maid came yesterday, I spoke to my husband. He spoke to the police. Even if he doesn't press charges, it's beyond his control. Once the crime is committed, it's up to the police… and the court… to decide.]
	WENDY	(*in Hokkien*) Ler eh lang jin ho. 让我们来你家…
15		虽然你有自己的困难,还对我们这么有耐心。 我真不能想你现这样 kang kor— (停顿) Thank you.
20		[You have been very kind… to allow us into your home… being so patient with us, despite your own… difficulties. I can't imagine what it must be like to go through such a horrible… (*slight pause*) Thank you.]
	MRS CHUA	不要告诉她。 [Don't tell her.]
25	WENDY	Sorry?
	MRS CHUA	你回到家后,当她问起我们见面的事,你就跟她说什么都没问题。告诉她…她不会有事的。
30		[When you get home, when she asks you how our meeting went, tell her everything will be fine. Tell her… she will be fine.]

WENDY 我知道她只是我的女佣但… 我不能欺骗她。
[I know she's my maid but… She doesn't lie to me, and I don't lie to her.]

ACT 1 : SCENE 4

Three weeks ago

In the following scene, the action takes place in different time and space. Melly enters wearing a long skirt and baggy t-shirt. She goes to her room. She changes to jeans and a tank top. Mrs Chua enters. She has a shopping bag. She is looking at clothes. Pause. Her phone rings.

MRS CHUA   Hello? Yes, I Mrs Chua… Hah? What accident?… 你可以说中文吗?
[Can you speak Mandarin?]
Slight pause.
I don't understand! I don't understand what you talking! Where Mr Chua?! What hospital?!… Okay, okay… Hello? Mr Chua, he die or no die?
Pause. She makes a call.

MRS CHUA   他受伤了! 是你的爸爸。哈? 我什么都不知道。有个印度人打了通电话给我。(装) You must come now. SGH. SGH (停顿) 你怎么大声做什么? 他是在联络所! 谁会要在联络所杀他呀? (停顿) Girl, 我… 我不知道应该穿什么。我得穿得体面一点, 对吗? 一定会有记者。要是他们问我问题怎么办? (停顿) 哎呀, 你啊! 我不是跟你说了吗, 我不知道! 那个印度人打电话给我, 那我就打电话给你。你爸现在是活还是死了, 我都不知道!
[It's your father! He's been hurt! Hah? I don't know anything. One Indian man called me. (*mimics*) You must come now. SGH. SGH. (*slight pause*) Why are you shouting? He was

at the CC! Who wants to kill him at the CC?
(*slight pause*) Girl… what should I wear?
Should wear something nice right? Surely
got reporters. What if they ask me questions?
(*slight pause*) Haiyah! I told you already,
I don't know! That Indian man called me,
now I'm calling you. Your father dead or not
I don't know!]
Mrs Chua hangs up. She exits. Pause. Melly's phone rings. She looks at it and answers. She speaks in Bahasa Indonesia.

MELLY   Aku sibuk, sayang… Aku nggak bohong, banyak kerja hari ini. Ma'am akan adakan acara makan malam. Semuanya dia mau aku masak. (*jeda*) MP?… Tapi ngapa malam ini sih? Kamu nggak bisa pergi hari lain—OK… Aku ngerti sayang, tapi aku nggak bisa tinggalkan rumah malam ini. (*jeda*) Kamu jangan khuatir yah, semuanya pasti OK. Kamu cuma jelaskan… beritahu MP bahwa kita berdua saling mencintai dan aku pasti dia akan berikan ijin untuk kita berdua langsung menikah! (*jeda*) Aku tau… Aku juga mau berada disitu… tapi malam ini betul nggak boleh. Kita jumpa besok yah?

[I'm busy, sayang… I'm not bluffing, I have a lot of work today. Ma'am is having a dinner party. She wants me to cook everything! (*pause*) MP? But why must you see the MP tonight? Can't you go another—Okay, I understand sayang, but I can't leave the house tonight.

(*pause*) Don't worry, it will be fine. You just tell the MP how much we love each other and he will allow us to get married immediately! (*pause*) I know... I also want to be there... but I really can't tonight. I see you tomorrow okay?]

Melly hangs up. She hears something. She puts on a baggy t-shirt and walks out. She sees Wendy, who is reading. They speak in Malay and Bahasa Indonesia.

MELLY   Ibu?

WENDY   Sudah time makan?
[Is it dinner time?]

MELLY   Belum. Melly... Melly perlu keluar sebentar.
[No, I'm... I need to go out for a while.]

WENDY   Okay...

MELLY   Trisha masih belum pulang... dan Sir katanya akan pulang lewat. Melly sudah siapkan makan malam. Nanti Melly panaskan bila Melly kembali yah.
[Trisha is not back yet... and Sir says he is coming home late. I've already made dinner. I'll heat it up when I come back.]

WENDY   Thank you Melly...

MELLY   Apa... Apa yang Ibu lagi baca itu?
[What... what are you reading?]

WENDY   Gua slalu tulis nota untuk Tony. Selit bawah pintu dia. Macam gini. (*she reads*) Tony the Chinese neighbours are making a lot of noise. Please call the Town Council. (*laughs*) Dia draw happy face sini. (*slight pause*) Ini brapa saja yang gua ada tinggal.

[I used to write notes for Tony. Slip them under his door. Like this. (*she reads*) Tony, the Chinese workers are making a lot of noise. Please call the Town Council. (*laughs*) He drew a happy face on this one. (*slight pause*) These are the only few I have left.]

MELLY   Ibu... Ibu OK nggak?
[Ibu... are you okay?]

WENDY   Gua OK. Jangan khuatir pasal gua Melly. Hari ini hari baik. Gua sudah habis baca baru punya buku. Gua tidur sikit... Hari ini hari baik.
[I'm fine. Don't worry about me Melly. Today is a good day. I finished reading a new book. I slept a little... Today is a good day.]

MELLY   Ibu... Sudah enam bulan semenjak Tony—
[Ibu... It's been six months since Tony—]

WENDY   Lu kata tadi mau kluar kan? Jangan kuat belanja ah! Check first sama gua kalau lu mau beli barang mahal.
[You said you were going somewhere? Don't spend too much money ah! Check with me first if you want to buy something expensive.]

MELLY   Melly tak perlu pergi skarang. Ibu mau Melly buat apa-apa?
[I don't have to leave now. Do you want me to do anything?]

WENDY   You are so sweet Melly. Kalau lu takda, gua tak tau apa gua bikin. (*laughs*) Kenapa lu pakai itu t-shirt so ugly? Kalau kluar sama kawan-kawan, lu mesti pakai cantik sikit.

[You are so sweet Melly. I don't know what I'll do without you. (*laughs*) Why are you wearing that ugly t-shirt? When you go out with your friends, you should wear something nice.]

MELLY   Nggak apa-apa, Bu.
[It's okay, Ibu.]

WENDY   At least comb your hair. Mari, gua tolong.
[At least comb your hair. Come, let me help you.]

Melly sits with Wendy, who combs her hair. Pause. Mrs Chua enters. She's carrying her husband's briefcase. She goes through his things. Her phone rings. She answers.

MRS CHUA   我到家了! 刚到家... 然后呢? 待在那里做什么? 他都还没醒过来? 他不会死的, 看他那张脸我就知道。(停顿) Girl, 你爸的PA问我有什么要告诉记者的吗? 他叫我上电视和记者说话... (停顿) 你为什么生我的气? 是他们问我的, 不是我问他们!

[I'm home! I'm home... Then? Stay there for what? He's not conscious... He won't die. I saw his face I know. (*slight pause*) Girl, your father's PA asked me if I want to say anything to the reporters. He asked me to talk to the TV, talk to the reporters... (*slight pause*) Why are you angry with me? They asked me you know, not I asked them!]

She hangs up. Pause. She puts on her jacket. She pretends to speak to the media.

MRS CHUA 谢谢! 谢谢你们的慰问。我的先生他会谢谢你们每个人的支持和祝福。(自言自语) 喂, 他还昏迷不醒。(停顿) 谢谢你们的慰问。我丈夫还在ICU但我们相信他会很快康复。他一向来都很健壮的。等他要是好一些回来后, 我打算我们一起去度假。可能会去中国。我想去探访我的祖辈的家乡。(停顿) 我要去探访我先生祖辈的家乡。(停顿) 我想他要是好一些回来后, 他一定会把我气到的半死。可是我还是会很敬爱他, 因为我始终是他的太太。(自言自语) 因为我始终是他的笨蛋太太。

[Thank you! Thank you for your questions. My husband would like to thank everyone for their support and well-wishes. (*to herself*) Eh, but he's not conscious yet. (*slight pause*) Thank you for your questions. My husband is still in ICU but we are hopeful that he will recover soon. He is a very strong man. When he gets better and comes home, we will go for a holiday. Maybe China. I want to visit my ancestor's village. (*pause*) I want to visit my husband's ancestor's village. (*pause*) When he gets better and comes home... he will drive me crazy but I will still love him because I am his wife. (*to herself*) Because I am his stupid wife...]

Pause.

MELLY Melly harus pergi Ibu.
[I should go Ibu.]

WENDY Ya, ya... Tunggu. Gua kasi lu cuba ini dress. Bukak lu punya t-shirt. (*jeda*) Bukak!

[Yes, yes… Wait. Let me give you a dress to try on. Take off that t-shirt. (*slight pause*) Take it off!]

Melly takes off the baggy t-shirt. We see her in jeans and the tank top.

WENDY   Ini kan cantik. Lu nampak sexy skali. (*tertawa*) Jangan kasi sembarang orang kacau lu OK?
[This is nice. You look very sexy. (*laughs*) Don't let anyone take advantage of you okay?]

MELLY   OK Ibu. Makasih… Ibu sungguh baik sama Melly.
[Okay Ibu. Thank you… You are so nice to me.]

WENDY   Lu kan family gua juga. (*jeda*) Eh lu nangis ah? Melly!]
[You are part of the family. (*slight pause*) Are you crying? Melly!]

Wendy is about to cry. She hugs Melly. Pause.

WENDY   You silly girl… Lekas balek.
[You silly girl… Come back soon okay?]

Melly goes to her room. Pause. Mrs Chua is still practising.

MRS CHUA   我先生是个非常热心的人，他一心一意花时间去帮助他选区的人。(停顿) 我知道他会好起来的。我告诉他出院后，要多休息，不要再那么辛苦。他呀，常常都在关心别人的问题。(停顿) 我问他，你的信念比你的生命重要吗？你的信念比我们这个家重要吗？(停顿) 我先生是我这一生见过的人之中最正直最无私的。谢谢。

[My husband is very passionate. He spends a lot of time helping people in his constituency. (*pause*) I know he will get better soon. I will

tell him, when you come home, you must rest. Don't work so hard. He is always worried about other people's problems. (*pause*) He has such strong beliefs. He always wants to help other people. I asked him before, are your beliefs more important than your life? Are your beliefs more important than your family? (*pause*) My husband is the most honourable and selfless man I have ever met. Thank you.]
Mrs Chua laughs. Melly makes a call. She speaks in Bahasa Indonesia.

MELLY   Eh pecun, lo dah siap belon? Gue tunggu lo di bawah lima menit lagi ye. Eh, abis gue dapet tuh $300 gue mau berhenti ah. Gak enak hati nih. Emak gue dah kelabakan. Calon gue bakalan ketemu MP dia nih malem, biar gue ama dia bisa kawin, eh gue malah di sini nyepong kontol Cina bau (*tertawa*) Abis malam ini, gue dah bisa kawin bo, akhirnya bisa jadi orang Singapur.
[Are you ready or not bitch? Okay, I see you downstairs in five minutes. Eh, today when I get $300 I want to stop already. I feel very bad lah. My Ibu is falling apart! My future husband is going to see his MP tonight, fighting for us to get married, and here I am sucking smelly Chinese cocks! (*laughs*) Eh… after tonight… I can finally get married… I can finally be a Singapore citizen.]

# ACT 2

ACT 2 : SCENE 1
Day 2

Melly is home. Pause. Wendy enters. They speak in Bahasa Indonesia and Malay.

MELLY   Ibu! Bagaimana? Apa kata Mrs Chua?
[Ma'am! How? What did Mrs Chua say?]

WENDY   Dia kata… semuanya akan jadi baik.
[She said… everything will be fine.]

MELLY   Oh iya? Dia bisa bantu? Dia bisa bantu Zul? Bisa nggak Melly jumpa sama dia nanti? Melly mau—
[Really? She can help? She can help Zul? Can I go and see him later? I want to—]

WENDY   Mrs Chua boleh cuba tolong. Tapi Zul sudah buat kesalahan. Dia masih akan dihukum.
[Mrs Chua can try to help. But he still committed a crime. He still has to be punished.]

MELLY   Iya… tapi mungkin… mungkin mereka tidak akan masukkan dia ke jail kan? Mr dan Mrs Chua akan maafkannya… jadi… jadi pengadilan tidak akan—
[Yah… but maybe… maybe they won't send him to jail right? Mr and Mrs Chua will forgive him… so… so the court won't—]

Melly's phone rings. She walks away and answers.

MELLY   Hello? Zul? Ibu, Zul ni! (*jeda*) Hah? Tapi… ngapa!? Kamu ada—
[Hello? Zul?! Ibu, it's Zul! (*slight pause*) Hah? But… why?! Did you—]

WENDY Kenapa?
[What's wrong?]

MELLY Katanya dia akan dimasukkan ke rumah sakit jiwa.
[He says they are sending him to the mental hospital.]

WENDY Mental hospital?

MELLY Hello? Zul? Hello!? (*jeda*) Ibu, gimanani… tolong…
[Hello? Zul? Hello! (*slight pause*) Ma'am, do something… please…]

WENDY Apa lagi lu mau gua buat Melly? Dia patut tau… kenapa dia tikam itu MP?
[What more do you want me to do, Melly? He should have known better than to stab an MP!]

MELLY Mereka tidak dengar cakap Zul. Dia diketawakan.
[But they didn't listen to him. They laughed at him.]

WENDY Tak ada siapa ketawakan dia.
[No one laughed at him.]

MELLY Zul bilang mereka ketawa, mereka tidak kasi ijin jumpa MP. Katanya MP juga tidak perdulikan dia. MP ada kerjaan yang lebih penting. Officer kata pada Zul, kenapa kamu mau kawin sama pembantu? Kamu pergi saja ke Batam, disana banyak. Kenapa mereka ngomong begitu?!
[Zul said they laughed, they didn't let him see the MP. He said the MP also brushed him aside.

| | | He said he had more important things to do. One of the people said to Zul, why you want to marry a maid? You can go Batam, got a lot there. How can they say that?!] |
| WENDY | Melly... Dengar cakap gua... Lu dekat sini, tinggal rumah gua. Gua jaga lu. Gua bilang sama lu skarang... lupakan dia... Lupakan saja sama dia. Kenapa lu mau ada mata air ni semua? Lu buang masa aja!
[Melly... listen to me... You are here, living in my house. I look after you. I'm telling you now... forget him. Just forget about him. Why do you want to get involved in relationships and all that? You're wasting your time!] |
| MELLY | Melly cinta dia.
[I love him.] |
| WENDY | Lu ingat lu cinta dia. Tapi nanti bila lu lepaskan dia, lu takkan cinta sama dia lagi.
[You just think you love him. After you let him go, you won't love him any more.] |
| MELLY | Tidak! Melly bukan seperti Ibu! Hanya karena Ibu tidak sayang Tony lagi—
[No! I'm not like you! Just because you don't love Tony any more—] |

Wendy slaps Melly. Pause.

MELLY Ibu tidak tangisi dia. Ma'am Margaret kadang telpon Melly, tanya Melly tentang Ibu... Apakah Ibu menangis, apakah Ibu sakit hati. Dia tanya Melly ngapa Ibu berhenti kerja, apa yang Ibu lakukan sepanjang hari...

1 [You never cry for him. Ma'am Margaret sometimes calls my handphone, asks me about you... whether you cry, whether you're in pain. She asks me why you stopped working, what you do all day...]

WENDY Abih?
[And...]

MELLY Melly bilang Melly tidak tahu apa-apa. Ibu selalu di dalam kamar Tony, dengan komputernya... (*jeda*) Ibu, Ibu selalu bantu Melly... Biarlah orang lain bantu Ibu juga...
[I tell her I don't know anything. You are always inside his room, with his computer... (*slight pause*) Ma'am, you help me so much... Let other people also help you.]

WENDY Ambik phone.
[Get me the phone.]

Melly gets Wendy's phone and passes it to her. Wendy makes a call.

WENDY Margaret, gua mo tukar gua punya handphone number, home phone number dan maid gua punya handphone number. Mulai skarang tak'a hubungan antara kita lagi. Dan gua tak mau tengok muka lu lagi slagi gua masih hidop. You are not welcome here. (*dia menutup telepon*) One less Christmas present to buy.
[Margaret, I am changing my handphone number, my home phone number and my maid's handphone number. There will be no more

contact between us from now on. And I don't want to see your face for as long as I live. You are not welcome here. *(she hangs up)* One less Christmas present to buy.]

She gives the phone back to Melly. Pause.

WENDY   Gua akan cakap sama lawyer pasal Zul kena masuk dalam hospital sakit jiwa.
[I will talk to the lawyer about Zul being in the mental institution.]

MELLY   Makasih Ibu.
[Thank you Ibu.]

WENDY   Lu jangan lagi sebut nama anak gua di depan gua.
[Don't you ever mention my son's name in front of me.]

Melly exits. Pause. Wendy goes to Tony's computer. She reads his conversation. Pause. She types.

ANGEL   Hello? Shishi?

SHISHI   Hey! Long time no see! You still changing the world?

ANGEL   I... I'm Angel's mother. His name is Tony. What's your name?

SHISHI   Hah?

ANGEL   My son... do you know him?

SHISHI   No lah... just chat only. Why? He in jail issit? LOL kidding.

ANGEL   No. He's...

SHISHI   Er, sorry Auntie. My mum calling me. Say hi to Angel/Tony 4 me k?

ANGEL   Shishi?

SHISHI   Yup?

ANGEL **My son killed himself.**

ANGEL **Do you know why?**

ACT 2 : SCENE 2
Day 14

Melly and Mrs Chua are at two separate realities. Melly is on the phone with Chitra.

MELLY Gue lagi nggak kepingin, pokoknya gue lagi nggak kepingin… (*jeda*) jam empat… satu lagi setengah enam… (*jeda*) gue nggak suka… gue memang benci bikin gini…
[I don't feel like it today. I said, I don't feel like it today! (*slight pause*) 4 o'clock… and another one at 5.30… (*slight pause*) I hate this… I just hate doing this…]

Pause. Melly changes into jeans and a tank top. Mrs Chua reads a newspaper headline.

MRS CHUA 一个热心的贤内助: 蔡忠敬太太
[STABBED MP'S WIFE: LOYAL PILLAR OF STRENGTH]

Pause. She goes through her husband's briefcase.

MRS CHUA (*reads*) Meet the People… App-li-ca-tion for Fi-nan-cial ass-is-tance. (*slight pause*) Not approved. Not approved. Not approved. (*slight pause. She writes on the form.*) Approve!

Pause. She makes a call.

MRS CHUA 喂? 老公啊? 你这些工作… 为什么每个都没被批准? 那人家见MP来做什么? 你只是在哪里做做样子而已, 对吗? (*停顿*) 是啦, 是啦, 你不要告诉我我不了解, 我比你了解地更清楚! 你知道外面有多少人在受苦吗? 我比你还更有能力帮他们! (*停顿*) 痛? 你已经在医院待了五个星期了!

每天说痛，痛，痛。不如你就留在那里啦，反正你的工作我还能比你做得更好!
[Hello, husband ah? All this work you do… why is everything not approved? Meet MP for what? Just show face is it? (*slight pause*) Yah lah, yah lah, don't tell me I don't understand. I understand better than you! You know how many people are suffering out there? I can help them better than you! (*slight pause*) Pain? You've been in hospital for five weeks! Every day pain, pain, pain. You just stay there. I can do your work better than you!]
She hangs up. She continues reading.

MRS CHUA Par-lia-ment Speech… We have done well with English as a common language. But over the years, due to new immigrants and foreign workers, we are seeing a shift… (*pause*)
We should uphold the ideals of our pledge "regardless of race, language—"

Pause. Melly and Mrs Chua have a conversation. Melly speaks in Bahasa Indonesia, Mrs Chua in Mandarin.

MELLY Seumur hidupku aku tidak punya apa-apa. Kedua orang tua ku bekerja di kota. Aku harus jaga saudara-saudaraku. Aku harus pastikan mereka tidak diculik atau dibunuh. Orang-orang di sini mengeluh melulu. Semua diprotes. Coba mereka tiggal di tempat dimana mereka tidak bisa ke sekolah, dimana mereka bisa diperkosa, mereka bisa dijual… dan kamu lihat apakah ada di natara mereka yang masih mengeluh melulu atau tidak.

[All my life I had nothing. My parents worked in the city. I had to take care of my brothers and sisters. I had to make sure they didn't get kidnapped or killed. People here always complain. Complain about everything. Try and grow up where they cannot go to school, where they can get raped, they can get sold… then you see whether you want to complain or not.]

MRS CHUA 我妈常跟我说,受教育是最重要的。她本身是南大的先锋学生… 那时是1958年。南大万岁,南大万岁。我还是记得,我还是个学生的时候。那时我妈妈常带我去上海书局… 在维多利亚街的那一间。她教我阅读,教我历史… 中国历史。中国文化。她说中国拥有五千年的文化历史。当我还是个少女时,我常问我妈妈,我们什么时候要回去中国呢? 我妈妈会笑着对我说,中国是过去的事。新加坡才是我们的未来。你很幸运。你生在新加坡的黄金时代。将来,大家会说,哇,新加坡有五千年的文化历史。而你,我的孩子,你就是新加坡的一分子。(停顿) 中国已经改变了太多了。现在新加坡很像中国,中国很像新加坡。不如两国就合为一国吧。一个富有但没有文化没有历史的国家。

[My mother always told me, education is the most important thing. She was a pioneer student at Nantah… back in 1958. Long live Nantah. Long live Nantah. When I was young, she used to bring me to the Shanghai Book Store at Victoria

Street. She taught me to read. She taught me history… Chinese history. Chinese culture. China has five thousand years of culture. When I was a young girl, I kept asking her, Ma, when are we going back to China? She would laugh. China is the past. Singapore is the future. You are very lucky. You are at the beginning of Singapore's golden age. In the future, people will say, wah, Singapore has five thousand years of history and culture. And you, my child, will be part of it. (*pause*) China has changed so much. Now, Singapore is like China. China is like Singapore. Might as well become one country. A new rich country with no culture and no history.]

MELLY   Kami sudah berancana untuk menikah tahun ini.
[We were planning to get married this year.]

MRS CHUA   为什么要浪费你的青春？结了婚又怎么样？不就等于变成他的免费佣人。
[Why waste your time? Get married and become what? Become his servant. You don't even get paid.]

MELLY   Aku bisa jadi rakyat Singapura.
[I can become a Singapore citizen.]

MRS CHUA   那有什么好处？
[What's so good about that?]

MELLY   Aku bisa jadi seperti kamu. Seorang wanita yang lebih hebat dari suaminya… lebih bijak, lebih kuat.
[I can be like you. A woman who is better than her husband… smarter, stronger.]

1	MRS CHUA	所以我就是喜欢你。我们是同类。
		[That's why I like you. We're very similar.]
	MELLY	Aku cuma lebih muda. (*jeda*) Aku tau kamu pikir bahwa aku tidak begitu cinta sama dia. Kamu pikir ini semuanya bohong. Tapi semuanya aku lakukan untuk dia… untuk kita, keluarga kita nanti. Aku yakin masa depanku cerah.
		[Except that I'm young. (*slight pause*) I know you think I don't really love him. You think it's a lie. But everything I do is for him… for us, our family. I have my future ahead of me.]
	MRS CHUA	未来？你还以为你和这个男人有未来吗？你又不是笨蛋，你明明知道他会在牢里蹲很久。你也知道你不会嫁给他。那你有什么打算？继续欺骗你的雇主，一个唯一关心你的人？还是打算找另一个新加坡男人，要他娶你？
		[A future? You still think you will have a future with this man? You're not stupid. You know he will be jailed for a long time. You know you will never marry him. What are you going to do next? Continue to deceive your employer—the only person who cares about you? Find another Singaporean man you can trick into marrying you?]
	MELLY	Aku datang ke sini untuk bekerja, untuk mencari uang karena… kenapa nggak? Mengapa aku nggak bisa dapat sedikit kesenangan? Mengapa aku nggak bisa punya fonsel yang bisa memainkan lagu kegemaranku? Mengapa nggak bisa keluargaku makan daging dan beli

pembakar roti dan punya kamar mandi?
Mengapa? (*jeda*) Aku bertemu dengan seorang
lelaki disini… dan walaupun dia hanya seorang
pembersih, dan walaupun kita tidak bisa
menikah, dia telah berjuang untuk aku. Dia
berjuang untuk aku! Apa yang suami kamu
telah lakukan untuk kamu?
[I came here to work, to make money
because… why not? Why can't I have some
little luxury? Why can't I have a nice phone
which can play my favourite songs? Why can't
my family eat meat and buy a toaster and have
a toilet? Why? (*slight pause*) I met a man here…
and although he's just a cleaner, and although
we can't get married, he fought for me.
He fought for me! What has your husband
ever done for you?]

MRS CHUA　给我滚回去。你不属于这里。他也不属于这里。回去印尼。回去马来西亚。全都回去。你们可以在这里工作，但你们不能留在这里。这个国家属于华人。我们的富裕是靠华人的本事，不是因为你的存在。你明不明白？
[Go back. You don't belong here. He doesn't
belong here. Go back to Indonesia. Go back to
Malaysia. All of you. You can work here, but
you can't stay here. This country belongs to the
Chinese. We are prosperous because of the
Chinese, not because of you. Do you understand?]

MELLY　For every action, there is an equal and
opposite reaction.

Melly walks away. Pause. Mrs Chua goes back to her files.

MRS CHUA   Not approve. Not approve. (*pause*) 在过几年，新加坡就会变成中国的首都。

[Not approve. Not approve. (*pause*) In a few years, Singapore will be the capital of China.]

ACT 2 : SCENE 3

Six months ago

In the following scene, the action takes place in different time and space. There is a projection of an online conversation between Tony (nick: angel) and an anonymous friend (nick: shishi).

ANGEL   Hey... I know your there.

ANGEL   C'mon...

ANGEL   Sorry bout last time.

ANGEL   Frens?

SHISHI   Wat u wan? Me busy.

ANGEL   Wan to say sorri. U ignoring me for days.

SHISHI   Cos you damn fucker.

ANGEL   Guilty.

Melly enters. She vomits. She is writing a letter. There is a shoebox next to her.

MELLY   Kepada... my... to... Sayang. Melly love... for you... (*pause*) To where you go I go... Melly miss for you. (*pause*) When we marry? Today I phone my family. They happy come Singapore. They... like Singapore money.

SHISHI   How's your song?

ANGEL   Sian. I read about these people, wat they're doing in their country...

SHISHI   Relak lah. Why care so much? You too free. No work ah?

ANGEL   Donno wat to do.

SHISHI   Wah lan, other people cannot find work, you want to pick & choose.

Melly's phone rings. She answers. She sings a song and laughs.

MELLY Tebak gue lagi ngapain? … Nggak lah! Elo tuh ya! *(tertawa keras)* Chitra, gue tuh baru muntah. Memek gue nyeri. *(tertawa)* Beneran. Parah banget lo! Tambahin lagi? Tapi dah gue taro kok. Iya deh, bentar…
[Guess what I'm doing? … No I'm not! You are! *(laughs loudly)* Chitra, I just vomited. And my vagina hurts. *(laughs)* It's true. You're so horrible… Put some more? But I put a few already. Okay wait…]

Melly puts some tablets into her vagina. Pause. She continues.

MELLY Yakin lo nih manjur? Kalau gue ampe mati, gue gentayangin lo ya! *(tertawa keras).* Gue bikin semua pelanggan lo kontolnya super gede trus maunya ngewein pantat lo. *(tertawa)* Nggak, gue gak bisa ketemu ntar… Gue mau ketemu Zul. Kayaknya dia mau ngelamar gue deh. Tapi kalo sampe nggak, gue dah punya rencana laen. Gue dah nulis SURAT CINTA buat tuh Cina… si supir taksi bangkotan! Kan dia dulu pernah bilang mo kawinin gue! *(dia tiba-tiba berteriak kesakitan)* Anjing… sakit banget! Gue ke dokter aja deh. Tapi… iya… iya… Gue istirahat aja… Nggak, belum keluar. Iya. Ntar gue taro di kotak trus gue buang ke luar. *(tertawa keras)* Lo ngangkang sana, dasar pecun karatan!

[Are you sure it'll work or not? If I die, I'll come back and haunt you. (*laughs loudly*) I'll make sure your clients will all have super big cocks and they want to fuck your asshole! (*laughs*) No, I cannot meet later... I'm meeting Zul. I think he's going to propose! But if he doesn't I have a back-up plan. I'm writing a LOVE LETTER to that Chinese man... that old taxi driver! He said before he wants to marry me what! (*she suddenly screams in pain*) Fuck, it's very painful. I better go doctor... There's no one at home! But it's—Okay, okay... I'll just rest... No, it hasn't come out yet... I'm going to put in a box and throw it outside. (*laughs loudly*) You go and spread your legs you old whore!]
Melly hangs up.

ANGEL   What for work? Take shit from other people. This country sux. Cannot do anything, say anything. People freakin robots and morons.

SHISHI   You damn slack la. Got education, dowan to find job, got maid to do everything for u

ANGEL   I just have to write one song and I can't even f-ing do that. I have to go.

SHISHI   Go where?

SHISHI   Wah lan, you always do this. F lah. I also gotta go.

SHISHI   Hey... Angel!

SHISHI   I feel like I'm bloody talkin to myself

Melly continues writing.

MELLY   Melly... Virgin for you. We... sex... Melly... first time. (*pause*) You sex Melly happy... When we marry... we sex every... time.

	ANGEL	Shishi?
	ANGEL	U there?
	ANGEL	Anyway... just wanted to say thanks.
	ANGEL	You're the best damn f-ing chat buddy – LOL
		I was going to type best chat f-ing buddy.
	ANGEL	I wish I could talk to you... Bye... I'm your f-ing guardian Angel

Melly lies down in pain. Pause.

	SHISHI	Hey, soz, Shishi went to HAHA shishi.
	SHISHI	Hey, wat u mean you want to talk... you fucking tryin to get my hp no out of me isit?
	SHISHI	Sorry man, I ain't fallin for that.
	SHISHI	Maybe... you gimme your hp no first... and a pic LOL. Then we see how...
	SHISHI	Cya later loser!

Wendy enters.

| | WENDY | I'm home! Dad's parking the car! Dinner will be ready in 10 minutes! Tony? Trish? |

Her handphone rings.

| | WENDY | Melly! Lu mana? Sudah pukul lapan. Lu lekas balek. (*dia menutup telepon*) [Melly! Where are you? It's 8 o'clock. Okay, okay... Come back soon. (*she hangs up*)] |

Wendy is outside Tony's room.

| | WENDY | Tony? Are you in there? Knock once for yes and twice for no. Tony? |

Pause. She enters the room. She freezes.

Melly aborts her foetus. She screams.

ACT 3

ACT 3 SCENE 1
Day 30

Wendy is with Mrs Chua. They speak in Mandarin and Hokkien.

WENDY 上次… 你说… (*in Hokkien*) Ler xi mi dai ji bun buay sai zo liao. 但是我真的很想帮忙我的佣人… [The last time… you said… this is out of your hands. But I really want to help my maid—]

Mrs Chua's phone rings. She answers.

MRS CHUA 喂? 我是蔡太太… 诶, 这么客气, 不用谢啦。呼吁信是我先生写的… 哦, 那就好。你的家庭真的应该得到政府的辅助。是啊, 当我读了关于你们经济情况的报道, 我就和我先生说—不好意思, 我有另一通电话。(停顿) 喂? 林医生! (笑) 应该是我谢谢你才对! 你真的是一位非常支持我们的议员! (笑) 政治… 不行, 政治不适合我。我能支持他就够了… 是的, 是的… 我们必须一起努力, 建立一个和谐社会。谢谢你… [Hello? Yes, this is Mrs Chua… No, please, you don't have to thank me. It's my husband who wrote the appeal letter… Oh, that's good. Your family really deserves financial assistance from the government. Yes! I read your case and told my husband that—Sorry, I have another call. (*slight pause*) Hello?… Dr Lim! (*laughs*) I should thank you! You have been the most supportive Minister! (*laughs*) No, politics is not for me. I just support him… Yes, yes… we have to work together to form community bonding. Thank you…]

She hangs up. Pause.

WENDY 我和她男朋友的 lawyer 谈过。那个 judge
很快就要 verdict 了。如果他坐牢,你的先生
可以去 MOM,叫他们让他们结婚呢?
我知道这不容易。

[I spoke to her boyfriend's lawyer. The judge
will give a verdict soon. Even if he goes
to jail, can your husband appeal to MOM
to allow them to get married? I know it's a
lot to ask.]

MRS CHUA 我想你应该有给她 off day 吧?
[Do you give her a day off?]

WENDY 只要她把工作做完,她想去哪里都没问题。
[She can come and go as she pleases. As long
as her work is done.]

MRS CHUA 你那么信任她。可是我听说有些女佣去芽笼赚钱。
很恐怖对吗? 有些女佣,她们只是想套住一个
新加坡人跟她们结婚,让她们就像是中马票一样,
变成有钱人。

[You trust her so much. I've heard of maids
working at Geylang to earn more money.
Terrible right? Some of these maids, they just
want to trap a Singaporean man into marrying
them so they can strike it rich.]

WENDY 变成有钱人? 她每个月的薪水只有 $300。她的
男朋友只是个 cleaner, 每个月的薪水才 $900。
[Strike it rich? She only earns $300 a month.
That man is a cleaner and earns $900.]

MRS CHUA 那他们要结婚做什么? 这样的条件怎么去组织
一个家庭。这些人就是有这种问题… 没有一点

责任感。你没有钱, 没学历, 那样怎么去养育孩子? 怎样去培养他们?

[Then why get married? How to start a family like that? That's the problem with all these people… no sense of responsibility. You have no money, no education, then your children how? How to support them?]

WENDY 那你是说穷人就不应该结婚?

[So you're saying poor people shouldn't get married?]

MRS CHUA 他们要怎么做, 都不关我的事。但是不要做一些事情, 然后要别人来帮他们。没有钱买房子, 就要求别人帮忙。没有钱养家, 就要求别人帮忙。什么事都要求别人帮忙, 要求别人帮忙…一点都不觉得羞耻。

[I don't care what they want to do. But don't go and do something, and then ask other people for help. You have no money to buy a house, you ask for help. You have no money to raise a family, you ask for help. Every day ask, ask, ask… They have no shame.]

WENDY 这不是我们社会里要做的duty吗?

[Isn't it our duty to help, as a society?]

MRS CHUA 我做了。我每天都在做。我捐给癌症机构, 儿童基金, 寺庙。我还捐给华乐团。大家还期待我做什么?

[I help. Every day I help. I give to cancer, I give to children, I give to temple. I even give to the Chinese Orchestra. What other help are people expecting from me?]

WENDY	我有说你的人很好。所以我只是要求你有点… compassion… 同情心。 [I know you are very generous. That's why I'm asking you to show some compassion.] *Pause.*
MRS CHUA	同情心… 当我的丈夫决定踏入政治圈,我的朋友们都拍着我的肩膀说:你现在富了。你将会得到很好的照顾。你将会得到很多好处。可是,没有人去想这些好处是要有一定的付出和限制的。我本来想要生三个… 或四个小孩。我想要两个儿子,因为我已经有两个女儿了。算起来我的大儿子今年就会29岁,另一个儿子会是27岁。也许其中一个今年会结婚。他们会组织自己的家庭… 他们的妻子都能享有毕业生妈妈的福利。(停顿) 这国家不是建立在同情心。而是看你有没有权势。我为了得到我现在的地位已经牺牲了很多。而我连VVIP的上层都还没达到。(笑) 那你呢? 你不期望得到更多吗? 还是你对你住在HDB组屋,四周围都是外劳的生活已经感到满足? [When my husband decided to enter politics, my friends patted my back. You will be rich now. You will be well taken care of. You will get all the incentives. No one realised that with incentives came restrictions. I had planned to have a third child… and a fourth. They would both be boys because I have two daughters. My elder son would be 29 now, and my younger son would be 27. Maybe one of them might get married this year. They can start their families…

Their wives can qualify for all these graduate mother incentives. (*pause*) This country has not been built on compassion. It's all about power. I've given up a lot to get where I am. And I'm not even at VVIP level. (*laughs*) What about you? Don't you desire more? Or are you content living in an HDB flat all your life, surrounded by foreign workers?]

WENDY 我的先生的工作很普通。他没有MP的benefits, 我也不象你, 我没有MP的太太的benefits。
[My husband has a simple job. He does not enjoy the perks of being an MP, and I don't enjoy the perks of being an MP's wife like you do.]

MRS CHUA (笑) 拜托, 只不过是议员而已。哪有这么厉害。你要做也可以做。议员。议员是做什么的? 就是对政府的任何提案表示支持。就是对民众的任何提问说无法支持。见民众。每个星期见民众。他妈的民众。每次我先生回到家都要喝五杯XO才可以睡觉。议员。你要做你拿去做。
(笑) 没关系的。我可以说这些话。我和我先生捐了很多钱给庙和和尚。他们一定会保佑我们的这一世还有下下一世。
[(*laughs*) Please lah MP only. As if so big. You want you can take. MP, do what? Say yes to everything the government ask. Say no to everything the people ask. Meet the People. Every week meet the People. Fuck the people. Every time my husband comes home he must drink five glasses of whiskey so that he can sleep. MP. You want you can take. (*laughs*)

It's okay, I can say these things. My husband and I pay the temple and monks a lot of money to make sure we will be taken care of for all our future lives.]

Melly is at another part of the stage. She looks at them.

WENDY 我是为我的女佣来的。她的男朋友不应该伤害你的先生的。但是你要明白那个 circumstances。没有人要听他说。那些人不让他见你的先生。他真的很 desperate 了。

[I'm here for my maid. Her boyfriend shouldn't have hurt your husband. But please understand the circumstances. No one was listening to him. They wouldn't even let him see your husband. He was desperate.]

MRS CHUA 他疯了！他是的危险的疯子。你知道疯子能干出什么吗？他们可能会去杀人，也可能自杀。(停顿) 你这是什么表情？你真的那么完美吗？是你自己毁掉你的家庭的，就别怪别人。

[He was crazy! He's a dangerous and crazy man. Do you know what crazy people do? They try to kill other people. Or they try to kill themselves. *(slight pause)* Why do you look so shocked? Are you that perfect? You ruined your own family's life. Don't blame others.]

WENDY You are everything I loathe in a human being.

MRS CHUA 你为什么讲英语？

[Why are you speaking in English?]

WENDY Because I can. Because English is my first language. I've demeaned myself by coming to see you again. How you barbarians become leaders of this country is beyond me. You have done nothing but cause trouble for us. You people are the filth of our society. So proud. Condescending. Sitting in your ivory tower, looking down at everyone, judging everyone. Laughing at everyone's suffering. Do you know what is going on around you? Do you know that people are happy your husband got stabbed? They say he deserved it. Because you have done nothing to help others.

MRS CHUA 你讲英语。你以为你有这个权利, 地位, 主导力。你看看。这些请求我们帮忙的申请书。什么经济补助。贫穷家庭。失业。驱逐通知。你以为这全都很容易处理, 是吗? 你做得到吗?
[You speak English. You think you have the right, the power, the leadership. Look at this. Request for help. Financial assistance. Needy family. Unemployed. Eviction notice. You think all this is easy to deal with? You think you can do it?]

Wendy grabs the papers and tears them.

WENDY 你妈是不是和他们一样? 她会不会是住在一房式组屋? 她会不会是在哪间咖啡店做清洁工人? 你看到她时, 会不会假装没看到? You can go on pretending to be the leaders of this country. You can go on pretending to care about the poor, the handicapped, the needy. But you people are a joke. A fucking joke. Despised by the very people you give your fucking hong baos to.

[Is your mother one of them? Is she living in a one-room rented flat? Is she working in a coffeeshop somewhere cleaning tables? Do you ignore her when you see her? You can go on pretending to be the leaders of this country. You can go on pretending to care about the poor, the handicapped, the needy. But you people are a joke. A fucking joke. Despised by the very people you give your fucking hong baos to.]

MRS CHUA　你为什么要来这里,为什么要求我帮忙?（笑）你要怎么帮你的佣人都可以。不过她不是那个需要你帮忙的人。你应该在精神病院,象你死去的儿子一样。

[Why are you here, begging for help? (*laughs*) You can do everything you want to help her. But she's not the one who needs help. You belong in a mental institution, just like your dead son.]

WENDY　When you have power, it doesn't matter what race you are, what language you speak. You will do whatever it takes to hold on to that power.

Mrs Chua exits. Pause. Melly goes to Wendy.

MELLY　Ibu. Melly perlu beritahu ibu sesuatu. Melly pernah ke sekolah dulu. Melly pernah belajar Bahasa Inggris... My English is very good, Ibu. I'm sorry... I'm sorry for lying to you. You have done so much for me. I don't want to lie to you any more... Maafkan Melly.

[Ibu... I have to tell you something. Last time I went to school. I studied English. My English

is very good Ibu. I'm sorry… I'm sorry for
lying to you. You have done so much for me.
I don't want to lie to you any more. Please
forgive me…]

ACT 3 : SCENE 2
Day 40

In the following scene, the action takes place in different time and space. Wendy is at home, looking at Tony's computer. Mrs Chua is at her home, on the phone.

MRS CHUA 是的,是的,他没事。那下次见民众是什么时候啊?可以把文件寄给我吗?恩,他一定会收到。我将会—我的意思是,他明天将会把全部的文件都做好。(停顿) 哦…下次开国会是什么时候? (停顿) 恩…他已经准备好要发言…我知道他从没发过言,你不用那么惊讶。你是他的PA,不是他的PM! (停顿) 哦…他的演讲是关于把华文列为全新加坡学生的必修课程。谢谢。 (停顿、自言自语) 凡事都将会改变。我的人生也将会改变。

[Yes, yes he's fine. When is the next Meet the People? Can you please send the documents to me? Yes, I will make sure he gets it. I'll finish— I mean, he will finish all the paperwork by tomorrow. (*slight pause*) Um…when is the next parliament sitting? (*slight pause*) Um… he has a speech prepared… I know he NEVER gives a speech. You don't have to sound so shocked. You are his PA not his PM! (*slight pause*) Um… his speech is about making Chinese Language compulsory for all Singaporeans! Thank you. (*pause. To herself*) Everything is going to change now. My life will change.]

She hangs up. She starts writing.

ACT 3 : SCENE 2

MRS CHUA 华人占了新加坡人口的绝大多数,而且还在不断增长。华人以他们的毅力与刻苦耐劳的精神建立了新加坡。但是,随着时间的冲击,某些政策慢慢地侵蚀了我们的文化与语言。我们必须尽力—

[The Chinese constitutes a majority of Singapore's population. And the Chinese population is still growing. The Chinese people have built Singapore with determination, diligence and hard work. However, over the years, certain policies have eroded our culture and our language. We must try to—]

Mrs Chua's phone rings.

MRS CHUA 嗯,那法官怎么说? 七年?!... 我知道他刺了你一刀,可是你又没死呀! (停顿) 那... 他们打算上诉吗?... (叹气) 只是一个小小的清洁工人,一生就这样完了。我为他感到伤心。(停顿) 为你感到伤心干吗? OK, OK, 我有很多工作要做。我等一下去医院—什么?! 什么时候? 明天?! 确定吗? 不过我以为医生不是说... 你要回家了,我当然开心啦。你不在时,我一直好寂寞。(停顿) 对呀... 一切都会回到跟从前一样的。

[Mm, so what did the judge say?... Seven years?!... I know he stabbed you but it's not as if you died! *(slight pause)* So... are they going to appeal?... *(sighs)* Just a simple cleaner and now his life is gone. I feel sad for him. *(slight pause)* Feel sad for you for what? Okay, okay, I have a lot of work. I'll go to the hospital later and— WHAT?! When? Tomorrow?! Are you sure?

But I thought the doctor said—... Yes, of course I'm happy you're coming home. I've been very lonely without you here. (*slight pause*) Yes... everything will go back to normal.]

Pause.

WENDY   I have done everything right—from the way I have brought up my children to the way I have treated my maid. I have done everything right.

MRS CHUA   是的,你做什么都是对的。我也是个母亲... 我做什么都是错的。
[Yes, you have done everything right. Just as I am a mother... and I have done everything wrong.]

WENDY   One less mouth to feed. One less child to worry about. I can sell this flat. Buy a house. That's what I've always wanted... My own house, with my own garden. (*slight pause*) I have done everything right... and from now on, everything right will be done to me. From now on, I'm going to have a good life.

Pause. Mrs Chua makes a call.

MRS CHUA   Hello, is this Chan Brother? I am Mrs— I am Madam Wong Lay Peng... I want to buy ticket... China. Only one... (*slight pause*) Return?

ACT 3 : SCENE 3
Day 50

In the following scene, the action takes place in different time and space. Melly is holding a shoebox. She is with Wendy.

WENDY   When you said you had lied... I didn't know what to think. That stupid Mrs Chua had put all kinds of terrible ideas into my head about you... Saying how some maids go to Geylang and work... or get pregnant... I felt as if I had lost faith... in everything... everyone.

MELLY   I have something for you Ibu... Please don't be angry with me any more...

She gives Wendy the shoebox. Wendy removes the lid. In the shoebox are hundreds of notes that she and Tony had written to each other.

MELLY   I kept them. I always found them when I was cleaning.

WENDY   All these notes! You saved every single one of them... Look at this! "Good luck for your exams Tony. You'll do great." I wrote this... two years ago! Melly, you are... you're a godsend!

MELLY   I want to go back home.

WENDY   Home? This is your home. Whatever problems you have, I can help and—

MELLY   Everyone is helping me... you... Mrs Chua... even Zul. That's why he's in jail. All I've done... all I've done... is just to help myself.

WENDY I know you're worried about Zul, but… whatever happens we can appeal.

MELLY I don't care about Zul. (*slight pause*) I don't love him. I thought I did. But I don't want to be with him. It's bad enough to be a maid. It's worse to be married to a cleaner. (*slight pause*) Please Ibu, let me go back…

Pause.

WENDY At the funeral… everyone was looking at me. Even Margaret said, why aren't you crying? That's your son. Why aren't you grieving? When people asked me, how are you… all I could say was, I'm okay. (*slight pause*) Is it wrong to be okay? Does it mean I don't love him. Yes, he's my son. Yes, he's dead. I know. I know. Because I just cremated him. (*slight pause*) I gave birth to him, I raised him… and I cremated him. I'm sorry if I didn't cry. I'm sorry if I didn't grieve the way you wanted me to. (*slight pause*) I did everything for Tony. I was his mother, his friend… I tried my best… and I couldn't save him. I don't even know… I don't even know why… (*slight pause*) And now… I can't save you. I can't have you.

MELLY He told me… he told me he loved you… more than anyone else. He wrote a letter… he said… don't give it to you.

Melly gives a letter to Wendy. They hug. Melly walks away and starts packing. Pause.

MRS CHUA 你可以不用读。
[You don't have to read it.]

1	WENDY	It's about time I did. It's about time I know…
	MRS CHUA	有什么需要知道的啊？什么需要明白的？(停顿) 里面是什么都不重要了。你的梦想… 你所有的期望… 你的想法 (停顿) 去加入联络所。参加基层活动。不久你会被尊重，被重视。你会成为一个模范公民。外表是那么完美的。(停顿) 里面到底是什么不是很重要的。
		[What is there to know? What is there to understand? (*slight pause*) What is inside is not important. All your dreams… all that you desire… all your thoughts… (*slight pause*) Go and join a CC. Take part in grassroots activities. Soon you will be respected and honoured. You will be an upright, model citizen. Perfect on the outside. (*slight pause*) What is inside is not important.
		Melly is packed and ready to leave. Pause.
	MELLY	Why are you going to China?
	MRS CHUA	他明天就要回来了。那我怎么办？我的生活又恢复正常了，跟从前一样正常。我明白为什么Wendy的儿子会自杀了。有什么比每天过这一样熟悉, 空虚的生活更可怕。
		[He's coming back tomorrow. What am I going to do with him? My life will just go back to normal, to how it used to be. I understand why Wendy's son killed himself. There's nothing worse than the familiar… living a familiar life, a vacant life.]
	MELLY	(*to Mrs Chua*) I thought I would be a Singapore citizen. Have a husband, children… a family.

I don't care if I have a small house. I don't care if we can't afford nice furniture. At least I will live here. My children will grow up here, go to school here. (*to Wendy*) That was my dream Ibu... That was my only dream...

MRS CHUA 那封信真的是他写的吗?
[Did he really write that letter?]

MELLY No. He left nothing. No note, no message... just his body. Dead... hanging...

MRS CHUA 你为什么要写?
[Why did you write it?]

MELLY She has done more for me than anyone else. She deserves... she deserves to be at peace.

MRS CHUA 这样你会比较安心对吗?
[Are you going to be at peace?]

MELLY I'm going to be at home.

MRS CHUA 我们的道德观念——像什么是对, 什么是错, 什么是好, 什么是坏... 什么是美德... 什么是良心。这些都只能从小培养 (停顿) Melly, 你是我一生中所遇到最有道德观的人。
[Our morals can only be inculcated when we are young. Knowing right from wrong, good from bad... understanding virtue... having a conscience. (*slight pause*) You, Melly, are the most moral person I have ever met.]

Melly exits. Pause. Mrs Chua exits. Wendy reads the letter.

WENDY Mum, I'm very sorry for what I've done. I'm not sad, and I don't want you to be sad.

I don't know who I am. I am strong. I am weak. There are people around me, in my life, loving me, caring for me. But I feel alone. I feel empty.

I don't want to start a new life. I don't want to talk to anyone. I don't want to run away. I just want to disappear.

I don't know who I am. But I know who you are—my mother.

You are everything good in life—hopeful, kind, generous.

You do everything. You sacrifice everything for us.

Mum, I am not worthy of life.

Please pray for me. Please pray for my eternal salvation.

Wendy keeps the letter in the shoebox. She smiles.

CURTAIN

NOTES

CHARACTER	CHARACTER

CHARACTER	CHARACTER

CHARACTER		CHARACTER	

CHARACTER		CHARACTER	

NOTES

NOTES

THEME	

THEME	

THEME	

THEME	

NOTES

NOTES

ABOUT THE PLAYWRIGHT

Haresh is Resident Playwright of The Necessary Stage and co-Artistic Director of the annual M1 Singapore Fringe Festival. To date, he has written 100 plays. One of these, *Off Centre*, was selected by the Ministry of Education as a Literature text for 'N' and 'O' Levels, and republished by The Necessary Stage in 2006. In 2008, *Interlogue: Studies in Singapore Literature, Vol. 6*, was published by Ethos Books. Written by Professor David Birch and edited by Associate Professor Kirpal Singh, it presents an extensive investigation of Haresh's work over the past 20 years. A collection of Haresh's plays was also translated into Mandarin and published as 哈里斯·沙玛剧作选 by Global Publishing. In 2012, Epigram Books reprinted *Those Who Can't, Teach*, which it first published in 2010.

Haresh was awarded Best Original Script for *Fundamentally Happy*, *Good People* and *Gemuk Girls* during the 2007, 2008 and 2009 *The Straits Times Life!* Theatre Awards respectively. In 2010, the abovementioned plays were published by The Necessary Stage in the *Trilogy* collection. Most recently, two collections of short plays by Haresh, *Shorts 1* and *Shorts 2*, were published as well. In 2011, Haresh became the first non-American to be awarded the prestigious Goldberg Master Playwright by New York University's Tisch School of the Arts.

ABOUT THE NECESSARY STAGE

Formed in 1987 by the current Artistic Director Alvin Tan, The Necessary Stage (TNS) is a non-profit theatre company with a charity status. Their mission is to create challenging, indigenous and innovative theatre that touches the heart and mind. TNS has been identified as one of the Major Arts Companies by the National Arts Council, and it is also the organiser and curator of the annual M1 Singapore Fringe Festival.

For its Main Season, TNS produces an average of two plays a year at the Black Box and other venues. The plays are original, mostly devised pieces created in a collaborative process involving research, improvisation (before scripting) and input from all members of the production.

The Necessary Stage shows its commitment to international exchange and networking through staging the company's plays abroad and inviting foreign works to be presented in Singapore, through dialogues, workshops and training opportunities, as well as through creative collaborations leading to interdisciplinary productions.

In addition, the TNS Theatre for Youth and Community branch actively engages young people, senior citizens and different communities in Singapore by conducting workshops and process-based drama programmes that focus on personal development.

ABOUT THE PUBLISHER

EPIGRAM BOOKS (epigrambooks.sg) is an independent publisher based in Singapore, established in 2011.

In addition to keeping in print fundamental literary texts through our Singapore Classics, Singapore Pioneer Poets and Playwright Omnibus series, as well as important translated works through our Cultural Medallion series, we firmly believe in consistently producing new writing of exceeding quality. This commitment can be found in our novels, poetry collections, playscripts and short story collections by notable writers such as Cyril Wong, Boey Kim Cheng, Tan Tarn How, Jean Tay and Mohamed Latiff Mohamed, as well as new voices such as Amanda Lee Koe (winner of the 2014 Singapore Literature Prize for Fiction), Jolene Tan and Justin Ker. *The Epigram Books Collection of Best New Singaporean Short Stories* biennial anthology series was started in 2013 to gather the best short fiction being produced by Singaporean prose writers.

We are also dedicated to children's literature, with bestselling and award-winning chapter book series such as *The Diary of Amos Lee, Danger Dan* and *Sherlock Sam*. Our picture books include the *Bo Bo and Cha Cha* and *Sam, Sebbie and Di-Di-Di* series, as well as Hedwig Anuar Award winners *Where's Grandma?* and *The Rock and the Bird,* and former President SR Nathan's *The Crane and the Crab*.

Our graphic novels include the Eisner-nominated *Monsters, Miracles & Mayonnaise* by drewscape, *The Art of Charlie Chan Hock Chye* by Xeric Award winner Sonny Liew, and the 25th Anniversary edition of *Tiananmen* by noted cartoonist Morgan Chua. And on the non-fiction front, we offer biographies of leading figures such as Chiam See Tong and Iskandar Ismail, compact coffee-table photography books, the Our Neighbourhoods series captured by Urban Sketchers Singapore and food books by the proprietors of Artichoke, Onaka and the Plusixfive Supper Club.